Impressum
Verlag: BABADADA GmbH, Nedderfeld 112 , 22529 Hamburg
Geschäftsführer / Verlagsleitung: Harald Hof
Druck: Books on Demand GmbH, In de Tarpen 42, 22848 Norderstedt

Imprint
Publisher: BABADADA GmbH, Nedderfeld 112 , 22529 Hamburg, Germany
Managing Director / Publishing direction: Harald Hof
Print: Books on Demand GmbH, In de Tarpen 42, 22848 Norderstedt

교실
classroom

나누다
divide

186/2

칠판
board

학교 운동장
school yard

교사
teacher

종이
paper

쓰다
write

펜
pen

책상
desk

자
ruler

책
book

학생
pupil

책가방
satchel

필통
pencil case

연필
pencil

연필깎이
pencil sharpener

지우개
rubber

스케치북
drawing pad

그림
drawing

붓
paintbrush

그림물감 통
paint box

가위
scissors

풀
glue

연습장
exercise book

숙제
homework

12

숫자
number

2+2

더하다
add

5-2

빼다
subtract

2×2

곱하다
multiply

계산하다
calculate

A

글자
letter

ABCDEFG
HIJKLMN
OPQRSTU
VWXYZ

알파벳
alphabet

hello

낱말
word

텍스트

text

읽다

read

분필

chalk

수업시간

lesson

출석부

register

시험

exam

증명서

certificate

교복

school uniform

교육

education

백과사전

encyclopedia

대학교

university

현미경

microscope

지도

map

휴지통

waste-paper basket

호텔
hotel

호스텔
hostel

환전소
bureau de change

여행가방
suitcase

자동차
car

언어

language

예 / 아니오

yes / no

좋아

Okay

안녕

hello

번역가

translator

고마워, 고마워요

Thank you

... 얼마입니까?

how much is...?

나는 이해하지 못합니다

I do not understand

문제

problem

안녕하세요!

Good evening!

안녕하세요!

Good morning!

잘자요!

Good night!

또 만나요

bye bye

방향

direction

수하물

luggage

가방

bag

배낭

backpack

손님

guest

방

room

침낭

sleeping bag

텐트

tent

여행 안내

tourist information

해변

beach

신용카드

credit card

아침식사

breakfast

점심식사

lunch

저녁식사

dinner

승차권

ticket

승강기

lift

우표

stamp

경계

border

세관

customs

대사관

embassy

비자

visa

여권

passport

여행 - travel

비행기
aeroplane

배
ship

소방차
fire engine

화물차
truck

버스
bus

모터보트
motorboat

자전거
bike

자동차
car

페리
ferry

보트
boat

오토바이
motorbike

경찰차
police car

경주차
racing car

렌트카
rental car

카셰어링

car sharing

견인차

breakdown truck

쓰레기차

refuse truck

모터

motor

연료

fuel

주유소

petrol station

교통 표지

traffic sign

교통

traffic

교통 정체

traffic jam

주차장

car park

기차역

train station

트랙터

tracks

기차

train

전차

tram

객차

carriage

헬리콥터

helicopter

공항

airport

타워

tower

승객

passenger

컨테이너

container

상자

carton

카트

cart

바구니

basket

출발하다 / 도착하다

take off / land

도시
city

마을

village

도심

city centre

집

house

영화관
cinema

광고
advert

가로등
street lamp

거리
street

택시
taxi

분식점
snack shop

보행자
pedestrian

인도
pavement

횡단보도
zebra crossing

쓰레기통
bin

교차로
crossing

신호등
traffic lights

CINEMA

오두막

hut

주택

flat

기차역

train station

시청

town hall

박물관

museum

학교

school

도시 - city

대학교

university

은행

bank

병원

hospital

호텔

hotel

약국

pharmacy

사무실

office

서점

book shop

상점

shop

꽃가게

florist's

수퍼마켓

supermarket

시장

market

백화점

department store

생선가게

fishmonger's

쇼핑 센터

shopping centre

항구

harbour

공원

park

벤치

bench

다리

bridge

계단

stairs

지하철

underground

터널

tunnel

버스 정류장

bus stop

바

bar

레스토랑

restaurant

우체통

postbox

도로 표지판

street sign

주차료 징수기

parking meter

동물원

zoo

수영장

swimming pool

모스크 사원

mosque

농장
farm

환경오염
pollution

공동묘지
graveyard

교회
church

놀이터
playground

절
temple

풍경
landscape

잎
leaf

이정표
signpost

길
way

초원
meadow

돌
stone

나무
tree

도보여행자
hiker

강
river

잔디
grass

꽃
flower

계곡
valley

산
hill

호수
lake

숲
forest

사막
desert

화산
volcano

성
castle

무지개
rainbow

버섯
mushroom

야자나무
palm tree

모기
mosquito

파리
fly

개미
ant

벌
bee

거미
spider

딱정벌레

beetle

개구리

frog

다람쥐

squirrel

고슴도치

hedgehog

토끼

hare

부엉이

owl

새

bird

백조

swan

맷돼지

boar

사슴

deer

순록

moose

댐

dam

풍력 터빈

wind turbine

태양광 전지판

solar panel

기후

climate

웨이터
waiter

메뉴
menu

의자
chair

수프
soup

피자
pizza

수저
cutlery

테이블보
tablecloth

전채요리

starter

주요리

main course

후식

dessert

음료수

drinks

음식

food

병

bottle

인스턴트 식품

fast food

길거리음식

street food

찻주전자

teapot

설탕통

sugar bowl

인분

portion

에스프레소 머신

espresso machine

높은 의자

high chair

계산서

bill

쟁반

tray

칼

knife

포크

fork

숟가락

spoon

찻숟가락

teaspoon

냅킨

serviette

유리잔

glass

접시
plate

수프 그릇
soup plate

컵 받침
saucer

소스
sauce

소금통
salt pot

후추통
pepper mill

식초
vinegar

기름
oil

양념
spices

케첩
ketchup

겨자
mustard

마요네즈
mayonnaise

수퍼마켓
supermarket

특가 판매
special offer

고객
customer

유제품
dairy

과일
fruit

트롤리
trolley

정육점

butcher´s

빵집

baker´s

무게가 나가다

weigh

채소

vegetables

고기

meat

냉동식품

frozen food

냉육

cold meat

통조림

tinned food

가루 세제

washing powder

달콤한 간식

sweets

가정용품

household products

세척제

cleaning products

판매원

salesperson

계산대

till

계산원

cashier

구매목록

shopping list

문 여는 시간

opening hours

지갑

wallet

신용카드

credit card

가방

bag

비닐 봉투

plastic bag

음료수

drinks

물
water

주스
juice

우유
milk

콜라
coke

와인
wine

맥주
beer

술
alcohol

카카오
cocoa

차고
tea

커피
coffee

에스프레소
espresso

카푸치노
cappuccino

바나나

banana

사과

apple

오렌지

orange

수박

melon

레몬

lemon

당근

carrot

마늘

garlic

대나무

bamboo

양파

onion

버섯

mushroom

견과류

nuts

국수

noodles

스파게티
spaghetti

쌀
rice

샐러드
salad

감자칩
chips

감자튀김
fried potatoes

피자
pizza

햄버거
hamburger

샌드위치
sandwich

커틀렛
cutlet

햄
ham

살라미
salami

소시지
sausage

닭
chicken

구이
roast

생선
fish

오트밀

porridge oats

뮤슬리

muesli

콘플레이크

cornflakes

밀가루

flour

크루아상

croissant

롤빵

bread roll

빵

bread

토스트

toast

비스킷

biscuits

버터

butter

응유

curd

케이크

cake

달걀

egg

계란 후라이

fried egg

치즈

cheese

아이스크림

ice cream

설탕

sugar

꿀

honey

잼

jam

누가 크림

chocolate spread

카레

curry

음식 - food

농가
farmhouse

헛간
barn

볏짚 더미
straw bale

들
field

말
horse

트레일러
trailer

트랙터
tractor

망아지
foal

당나귀
donkey

새끼 양
lamb

양
sheep

염소

goat

암소

cow

송아지

calf

돼지

pig

새끼 돼지

piglet

황소

bull

거위

goose

오리

duck

병아리

chick

암탉

hen

수탉

cock

쥐

rat

고양이

cat

생쥐

mouse

황소

ox

개

dog

개집

doghouse

정원용 호스

garden hose

물뿌리개

watering can

큰 낫

scythe

쟁기

plough

낫
sickle

괭이
hoe

쇠스랑
pitchfork

도끼
axe

외바퀴 손수레
wheelbarrow

여물통
trough

우유 캔
milk can

부대
sack

울타리
fence

축사
stable

비닐하우스
greenhouse

땅
soil

씨앗
seed

거름
fertilizer

콤바인
combine harvester

수확하다

harvest

수확

harvest

참마

yams

밀

wheat

콩

soy

감자

potato

옥수수

corn

유채씨

rapeseed

과일나무

fruit tree

카사바

cassava

곡식

cereals

굴뚝
chimney

지붕
roof

낙수 홈통
drainpipe

창문
window

차고
garage

초인종
doorbell

문
door

쓰레기통
rubbish bin

우편함
letterbox

정원
garden

응접실

living room

옥실

bathroom

부엌

kitchen

침실

bedroom

아이들 방

child's room

식사실

dining room

바닥

floor

벽

wall

천장

ceiling

지하실

cellar

사우나

sauna

발코니

balcony

테라스

terrace

수영장

pool

잔디 깎는 기계

lawn mower

침대 시트

sheet

이불

bedspread

침대

bed

빗자루

broom

양동이

bucket

스위치

switch

벽지
wallpaper

그림
picture

전등
lamp

선반
shelf

캐비닛
cupboard

벽난로
fireplace

텔레비전
television

꽃
flower

쿠션
cushion

꽃병
vase

소파
sofa

리모컨
remote control

카페트

carpet

커튼

curtain

탁자

table

의자

chair

흔들의자

rocking chair

안락의자

armchair

책
......
book

담요
......
blanket

장식
......
decoration

뗄감나무
......
firewood

영화
......
film

하이파이 기기
......
hi-fi equipment

열쇠
......
key

신문
......
newspaper

회화
......
painting

포스터
......
poster

라디오
......
radio

노트
......
notepad

진공청소기
......
hoover

선인장
......
cactus

초
......
candle

냉장고
fridge

전자레인지
microwave oven

주방용 저울
kitchen scales

세척제
detergent

토스터
toaster

오븐
oven

냉동실
freezer

쓰레기통
rubbish bin

식기세제
dishwasher

쿠커

cooker

냄비

pot

주철 냄비

cast-iron pot

웍 / 카다이 냄비

wok / kadai

프라이팬

pan

주전자

kettle

찜기
steamer

오븐 구이용 쟁반
baking tray

그릇
crockery

머그
mug

양푼이
bowl

젓가락
chopsticks

국자
ladle

주걱
spatula

거품기
whisk

여과기
strainer

체
sieve

강판
grater

절구
mortar

바베큐
barbecue

화덕
open fire

도마
chopping board

밀방망이
rolling pin

코르크 병따개
corkscrew

캔
can

캔 따개
can opener

냄비 받침
pot holder

개수대
sink

솔
brush

수세미
sponge

블렌더
blender

냉동고
deep freezer

젖병
baby bottle

수도꼭지
tap

히터
heating

수건
towel

샤워
shower

거품 비누
bubble bath

샤워 커튼
shower curtain

옥조
bathtub

유리잔
glass

세탁기
washing machine

타일
tiles

수도꼭지
tap

변기
potty

개수대
sink

화장실
toilet

재래식 화장실
squat toilet

비데
bidet

공중 변소
urinal

화장지
toilet paper

변기솔
toilet brush

치솔
toothbrush

치약
toothpaste

치실
dental floss

씻다
wash

샤워기
handheld shower

질 세척제
douche

대야
basin

등밀이솔
back brush

비누
soap

샤워 젤
shower gel

샴푸
shampoo

물걸레
flannel

배수관
drain

크림
cream

체취 제거제
deodorant

거울

mirror

휴대용 거울

hand mirror

면도기

razor

면도 거품

shaving foam

에프터쉐이브

aftershave

빗

comb

솔

brush

헤어드라이기

hair dryer

헤어스프레이

hairspray

메이크업

makeup

립스틱

lipstick

손톱깎이

nail varnish

면 솜

cotton wool

손톱

nail scissors

향수

perfume

세면도구 주머니

washbag

스툴

stool

저울

weighing scale

목욕 가운

bathrobe

고무 장갑

rubber gloves

탐폰

tampon

생리대

sanitary towel

화학 화장실

chemical toilet

자명종
alarm clock

털인형
cuddly toy

장난감 차
toy car

인형의 집
doll's house

선물
present

딸랑이
rattle

풍선
balloon

침대
bed

유모차
pram

카드 게임
deck of cards

퍼즐
jigsaw

만화
comic

레고

lego bricks

장난감 블럭

building blocks

액션 캐릭터

action figure

베이비 그로

babygrow

프리스비

frisbee

모빌

mobile

보드 게임

board game

주사위

dice

기차 모형 세트

model train set

노리개 젖꼭지

dummy

파티

party

그림책

picture book

공

ball

인형

doll

놀다

play

모래상자

sandpit

그네

swing

장난감

toys

비디오 게임 콘솔

video game console

세바퀴자전거

tricycle

곰인형

teddy bear

옷장

wardrobe

의복
clothing

양말

socks

스타킹

stockings

스타킹

tights

스카프
scarf

우산
umbrella

티셔츠
t-shirt

허리띠
belt

부츠
boots

슬리퍼
slippers

운동화
trainers

샌들
sandals

신발
shoes

고무 장화
rubber boots

팬티
underpants

브래지어
bra

러닝 셔츠
vest

의복 - clothing

바디
body

바지
trousers

청바지
jeans

치마
skirt

블라우스
blouse

셔츠
shirt

풀오버
pullover

후드티
hoodie

블레이저
blazer

자켓
jacket

외투
coat

비옷
raincoat

의상
costume

원피스
dress

웨딩 드레스
wedding dress

양복

suit

나이트가운

nightgown

잠옷

pyjamas

사리

sari

두건

headscarf

터번

turban

부르카

burqa

카프탄

kaftan

아바야

abaya

수영복

swimsuit

수영바지

trunks

반바지

shorts

트레이닝복

tracksuit

앞치마

apron

장갑

gloves

단추

button

안경

glasses

팔찌

bracelet

목걸이

necklace

반지

ring

귀걸이

earring

캡 모자

cap

옷걸이

coat hanger

모자

hat

넥타이

tie

지퍼

zip

헬멧

helmet

멜빵

braces

교복

school uniform

유니폼

uniform

턱받이
bib

노리개 젖꼭지
dummy

기저귀
nappy

서버
server

서류 캐비닛
filing cabinet

인쇄기
printer

종이
paper

모니터
monitor

책상
desk

마우스
mouse

폴더
folder

자판기
keyboard

휴지통
waste-paper basket

컴퓨터
computer

의자
chair

커피잔
coffee mug

계산기
calculator

인터넷
internet

노트북

laptop

편지

letter

메시지

message

휴대전화

mobile

네트워크

network

복사기

photocopier

소프트웨어

software

전화

telephone

플러그 소켓

plug socket

팩시밀리

fax machine

서식

form

서류

document

사다

buy

지불하다

pay

거래하다

trade

돈

money

달러

dollar

유로

euro

엔

yen

루벨

rouble

스위스 프랑

Swiss franc

위안

renminbi yuan

루피

rupee

현금인출기

cashpoint

환전소

bureau de change

금

gold

은

silver

석유

oil

에너지

energy

가격

price

계약

contract

세금

tax

주식

stock

일하다

work

근로자

employee

고용주

employer

공장

factory

상점

shop

경찰관
police officer

소방관
fireman

요리사
cook

의사
doctor

조종사
pilot

정원사

gardener

목수

carpenter

수선공

seamstress

판사

judge

화학자

chemist

배우

actor

버스운전사

bus driver

택시 운전사

taxi driver

어부

fisherman

청소부

cleaning lady

지붕 수리자

roofer

웨이터

waiter

사냥꾼

hunter

화가

painter

제빵사

baker

전기업자

electrician

건축업자

builder

엔지니어

engineer

정육점업자

butcher

배관업자

plumber

우편물 배달부

postman

군인

soldier

건축가

architect

계산원

cashier

플로리스트

florist

미용사

hairdresser

검표원

conductor

정비사

mechanic

선장

captain

치과의사

dentist

학자

scientist

유대교 라비

rabbi

이맘

imam

수도승

monk

사제

clergyman

망치
hammer

펜치
pliers

나사 드라이버
screwdriver

렌치
spanner

손전등
torch

굴삭기

digger

연장통

toolbox

사다리

ladder

톱

saw

못

nails

드릴

drill

수리하다
repair

삽
shovel

젠장!
Damn!

쓰레받기
dustpan

페인트통
paint pot

나사
screws

악기
musical instruments

드럼
drum kit

스피커
loudspeaker

콘트라베이스
double bass

트럼펫
trumpet

기타
guitar

피아노

piano

바이올린

violin

베이스

bass

팀파니

timpani

북

drums

키보드

keyboard

색소폰

saxophone

플루트

flute

마이크

microphone

입구
entrance

호랑이
tiger

우리
cage

얼룩말
zebra

사료
animal feed

판다 곰
panda

동물

animals

코끼리

elephant

캥거루

kangaroo

코뿔소

rhino

고릴라

gorilla

곰

bear

낙타

camel

타조

ostrich

사자

lion

원숭이

monkey

홍학

flamingo

앵무새

parrot

북극곰

polar bear

펭귄

penguin

상어

shark

공작

peacock

뱀

snake

악어

crocodile

동물원 사육사

zookeeper

물개

seal

재규어

jaguar

조랑말

pony

표범

leopard

하마

hippo

기린

giraffe

독수리

eagle

맷돼지

boar

생선

fish

거북이

turtle

바다코끼리

walrus

여우

fox

영양

gazelle

미식축구
American football

자전거
경기
cycling

테니스
tennis

농구
basketball

수영
swimming

권투
boxing

아이스하키
ice hockey

축구

football

배드민턴

badminton

육상 경기

athletics

핸드볼

handball

스키

skiing

폴로

polo

뛰어오르다
jump

옷다
laugh

포옹하다
hug

걷다
walk

노래하다
sing

기도하다
pray

입맞추다
kiss

꿈꾸다
dream

쓰다
write

그리다
draw

보여주다
show

밀다
push

주다
give

받다
take

가지다
have

행하다
do

...이다
be

서있다
stand

뛰다
run

당기다
pull

던지다
throw

떨어지다
fall

누워있다
lie

기다리다
wait

운반하다
carry

앉다
sit

옷을 입다
get dressed

자다
sleep

깨다
wake up

보다

look at

울다

cry

쓰다듬다

stroke

빗다

comb

말하다

talk

이해하다

understand

묻다

ask

듣다

listen

마시다

drink

먹다

eat

정리하다

tidy up

사랑하다

love

요리하다

cook

주행하다

drive

날다

fly

활동 - activities

해항하다

sail

계산하다

calculate

읽다

read

배우다

learn

일하다

work

결혼하다

marry

바느질하다

sew

이를 닦다

brush teeth

죽이다

kill

담배 피우다

smoke

보내다

send

할머니
grandmother

할아버지
grandfather

아버지
father

어머니
mother

아기
baby

딸
daughter

아들
son

손님

guest

이모 / 고모

aunt

삼촌

uncle

형제

brother

자매

sister

이마
forehead

눈
eye

어깨
shoulder

손가락
finger

얼굴
face

턱
chin

손가락
hand

가슴
breast

다리
leg

팔
arm

아기

baby

남자

man

여자

woman

소녀

girl

소년

boy

머리카락

head

등

back

배

belly

배꼽

belly button

발가락

toe

발꿈치

heel

뼈

bone

엉덩이

hip

무릎

knee

팔꿈치

elbow

코

nose

둔부

bottom

피부

skin

뺨

cheek

귀

ear

입술

lip

입
mouth

치아
tooth

혀
tongue

뇌
brain

심장
heart

근육
muscle

허파
lung

간
liver

위
stomach

신장
kidneys

성교
sex

콘돔
condom

난자
ovum

정자
semen

임신
pregnancy

월경
menstruation

질
vagina

음경
penis

눈썹
eyebrow

머리카락
hair

목
neck

몸통 - body

병원
hospital

병원
hospital

구급차
ambulance

휠체어
wheelchair

골절
fracture

의사

doctor

응급실

emergency room

간호사

nurse

응급상황

emergency

혼수상태

unconscious

통증

pain

부상

injury

출혈

bleeding

심장마비

heart attack

뇌졸중

stroke

알러지

allergy

기침

cough

열

fever

독감

flu

설사

diarrhoea

두통

headache

암

cancer

당뇨병

diabetes

외과의

surgeon

수술용 메스

scalpel

수술

operation

병원 - hospital

73

CT

CT

엑스레이

x-ray

초음파

ultrasound

마스크

face mask

질병

disease

대기실

waiting room

목발

crutch

반창고

plaster

붕대

bandage

주사

injection

청진기

stethoscope

들것

stretcher

체온계

clinical thermometer

출생

birth

과체중

overweight

보청기

hearing aid

소독약

disinfectant

감염

infection

바이러스

virus

HIV / AIDS

HIV / AIDS

의학

medicine

예방접종

vaccination

알약

tablets

알약

pill

구급 전화

emergency call

혈압측정기

blood pressure monitor

병든 / 건강한

ill / healthy

도와주세요!

Help!

경보음

alarm

폭행

assault

공격

attack

위험

danger

비상구

emergency exit

불이야!

Fire!

소화기

fire extinguisher

사고

accident

구급 상자

first-aid kit

SOS

SOS

경찰

police

유럽

Europe

북미

North America

남미

South America

아프리카

Africa

아시아

Asia

호주

Australia

북극

Atlantic

태평양

Pacific

인도양

Indian Ocean

남극해

Antarctic Ocean

북극해

Arctic Ocean

북극해

North Pole

남극해

South Pole

남극

Antarctica

지구

Earth

육지

land

바다

sea

섬

island

국가

nation

주

state

시계 문자판

clock face

시침

hour hand

분침

minute hand

초침

second hand

몇 시입니까?

What time is it?

일

day

시간

time

지금

now

디지털 시계

digital watch

분

minute

시간

hour

월요일 Monday
화요일 Tuesday
수요일 Wednesday
목요일 Thursday
금요일 Friday
토요일 Saturday
일요일 Sunday

어제
yesterday

오늘
today

내일
tomorrow

아침
morning

정오
noon

저녁
evening

근로일
business days

주말
weekend

비
rain

무지개
rainbow

바람
wind

눈
snow

봄
spring

여름
summer

가을
autumn

겨울
winter

날씨 예보

weather forecast

온도계

thermometer

햇빛

sunshine

구름

cloud

안개

fog

습도

humidity

번개

lightning

천둥

thunder

폭풍

storm

우박

hail

장마

monsoon

홍수

flood

얼음

ice

1월

January

2월

February

3월

March

4월

April

5월

May

6월

June

7월

July

8월

August

9월
September

10월
October

11월
November

12월
December

형태
shapes

원
circle

정사각형
square

직사각형
rectangle

삼각형
triangle

구
sphere

정사면체
cube

하양

white

노랑

yellow

주황

orange

분홍

pink

빨강

red

보라

purple

파랑

blue

초록

green

갈색

brown

회색

grey

검정

black

많은 / 적은

a lot / a little

화난 / 차분한

angry / calm

아름다운 / 추한

beautiful / ugly

시작 / 끝

beginning / end

큰 / 작은

big / small

밝은 / 어두운

bright / dark

형제 / 자매

brother / sister

깨끗한 / 더러운

clean / dirty

완전한 / 불완전한

complete / incomplete

낮 / 밤

day / night

죽은 / 산

dead / alive

넓은 / 좁은

wide / narrow

삭용의 / 비식용의

edible / inedible

불친절한 / 친절한

evil / kind

흥분된 / 지루한

excited / bored

뚱뚱한 / 마른

fat / thin

처음으로 / 마지막으로

first / last

친구 / 적

friend / enemy

꽉 찬 / 텅 빈

full / empty

딱딱한 / 부드러운

hard / soft

무거운 / 가벼운

heavy / light

배고픔 / 목마름

hunger / thirst

병든 / 건강한

ill / healthy

불법 / 합법

illegal / legal

영리한 / 어리석은

intelligent / stupid

왼 / 오른

left / right

가까운 / 먼

near / far

새 / 헌

new / used

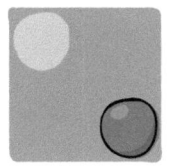

무 / 유

nothing / something

늙은 / 젊은

old / young

온 / 오프

on / off

열린 / 닫힌

open / closed

조용한 / 시끄러운

quiet / loud

부유한 / 가난한

rich / poor

옳은 / 틀린

right / wrong

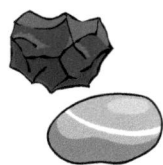

거친 / 매끄러운

rough / smooth

슬픈 / 기쁜

sad / happy

짧은 / 긴

short / long

느린 / 빠른

slow / fast

젖은 / 마른

wet / dry

따뜻한 / 시원한

warm / cool

전쟁 / 평화

war / peace

반대 - opposites

0	**1**	**2**
영	하나	둘
zero	one	two

3	**4**	**5**
셋	넷	다섯
three	four	five

6	**7**	**8**
여섯	일곱	여덟
six	seven	eight

9	**10**	**11**
아홉	열	열하나
nine	ten	eleven

12
열둘

twelve

13
열셋

thirteen

14
열넷

fourteen

15
열다섯

fifteen

16
열여섯

sixteen

17
열일곱

seventeen

18
열여덟

eighteen

19
열아홉

nineteen

20
스물

twenty

100
백

hundred

1.000
천

thousand

1.000.000
백만

million

영어
....
English

미국식 영어
....
American English

중국어 만다린
....
Chinese Mandarin

힌두어
....
Hindi

스페인어
....
Spanish

프랑스어
....
French

아랍어
....
Arabic

러시아어
....
Russian

포르투갈어
....
Portuguese

불가리아어
....
Bengali

독일어
....
German

일본어
....
Japanese

나

I

너

you

그 / 그녀/ 그것

he / she / it

우리

we

너희들

you

그들

they

누가?

who?

무엇이?

what?

어떻게?

how?

어디서?

where?

언제?

when?

이름

name

어디에
where

두이에

behind

안에

in

앞에

in front of

위에

over

위에

on

아래에

under

옆에

beside

사이에

between

장소

place